On the Road

The Volkswagen Beetle

by Linda Jean Lally

Consultant:
Lee W. Kopotic
Member
VW Club of America

RiverFront Books

an imprint of Franklin Watts
A Division of Grolier Publishing
New York   London   Hong Kong   Sydney
Danbury, Connecticut

J E 29.2222
Lal

120688

RiverFront Books
http://publishing.grolier.com

Library of Congress Cataloging-in-Publication Data
Lally, Linda.
    The Volkswagen Beetle/by Linda Lally.
    p. cm.—(On the road)
    Includes bibliographical references (p. 44) and index.
    Summary: Traces the history, development, and design of the popular
bug-shaped car, from its origins in Nazi Germany, to its appeal among college
students in the 1960s, to its nostalgic but modern version introduced in 1998.
    ISBN 0-7368-0185-5
    1. Volkswagen Beetle automobile—History—Juvenile literature.
[1. Volkswagen Beetle automobile.] I. Title. II. Series: On the road
(Mankato, Minn.)
TL215.V6L35 1999
629.222'2—dc21   98-48552
                                                                      CIP
                                                                       AC

Editorial Credits
Blake Hoena, editor; Timothy Halldin, cover designer; Linda Clavel, illustrator;
    Kimberly Danger and Sheri Gosewisch, photo researchers

Photo Credits
Corbis-Bettman/UPI, 45
Corbis/Library of Congress, 10; Hulton-Deutsch Collection, 13;
    Austrian Archives, 14
Impact Visuals/Jim West, cover, 4, 8, 26, 41
Ronald Cantor, 17
Ron Kimball, 20, 24, 29, 31, 32–33
Transparencies, Inc./J. G. Faircloth, 7, 30
Unicorn Stock Photos/Paul A. Hein, 23
Visuals Unlimited/Emily Stong, 18, 37

Table of Contents

Chapter 1

The Volkswagen Beetle

In 1994, a German automaker introduced a new car at car shows. This automaker was Volkswagen. Volkswagen called its new car Concept 1.

Concept 1 was a concept car. Concept cars display the design ideas automakers have for new car models. Automakers display these cars at car shows to see if the public likes them. The public's opinion often helps automakers decide whether to mass-produce concept cars. Automakers usually only make cars in large quantities if the public likes them.

Volkswagen first displayed Concept 1 at the North American International Auto Show in Detroit, Michigan.

The public did not think Concept 1 was a completely new car idea. They thought Volkswagen was remaking an old car model called the Beetle. The Beetle was originally designed in the 1930s by Ferdinand Porsche. It was one of the most popular cars ever made.

The Designer of the Original Beetle

Ferdinand Porsche was talented at working with electricity. In 1898, Jacob Lohner & Company hired Porsche. This company made horse-drawn coaches. But the company's owner thought electric cars would replace coaches. In 1900, Porsche designed his first car for this company. This car was called the Lohner-Porsche Chaise.

In 1930, Porsche started his own car design company. He showed one of his small car designs to Adolf Hitler in 1934. Hitler was the leader of Germany. At the time, Hitler wanted a cheap and dependable car for the German people. He hired Porsche to build this car. Hitler called the car Volkswagen. Volkswagen means "people's car" in German. Later, the

Ferdinand Porsche designed the original Beetle in the 1930s.

Volkswagen became known as the Beetle. It had a rounded back. People thought it looked like a bug.

Concept 1

Concept 1 reminded people of the Beetle. But at first, Volkswagen officials denied that Concept 1 was a remake of the original Beetle. They said

The public thought Concept 1 was a new model of the Volkswagen Beetle.

Concept 1 was only a design experiment. Volkswagen officials also said that this car probably would not be mass-produced.

Concept 1 and the Beetle had similar designs. Both cars had small, rounded bodies. They both were two-door coupes. A coupe is a car with two doors and a hard roof. Both cars also had similar dashboards with one round speedometer. A speedometer shows drivers how fast they are driving.

The public liked Concept 1. Volkswagen officials then admitted that this car really was a remake of the old Beetle. They said Concept 1 was the first prototype. This car was a test model of the new Beetle that Volkswagen planned to build. In 1998, Volkswagen started mass-producing the new Beetle.

Volkswagen made many changes to the new Beetle. The old Beetle had its engine in the rear of the car. The new Beetle has its engine in the front of the car. The old Beetle had rear-wheel drive. Power from the engine turned the rear wheels. The new Beetle has front-wheel drive. Power from the engine turns the front wheels.

The new Beetle also has options the old Beetle did not have. Options are extra features. The new Beetle has air conditioning, a CD player, and heated seats.

Chapter 2

Inventing the Beetle

Ferdinand Porsche dreamed of building a small car. In the 1920s, he designed the Type 130 while working for Austrian automaker Daimler-Benz. But this company made big luxury cars. Daimler-Benz did not want to build small cars.

In 1930, Porsche started his own company to continue his work on a small car design. He called his company the Porsche Bureau.

In 1932, the owner of Zündapp Works asked Porsche's company to design a small car. Zündapp Works built motorcycles in Nürnberg, Germany. But motorcycles were not selling well. Zündapp Works wanted to produce a small car it could sell.

The Beetle was the most successful small car Ferdinand Porsche designed.

The car Porsche designed was called Project 12. Prototypes of this car were built in 1932. These test models of Project 12 had two doors and their engines were in the rear of the car. But Zündapp Works did not mass-produce Project 12 cars. Porsche was having problems with the design of the engine. It kept breaking down. Also, motorcycle sales began to improve at this time. For these reasons, Zündapp Works decided not to build Project 12 cars. Instead, the company continued to make only motorcycles.

Adolf Hitler and Ferdinand Porsche

In 1934, Porsche was working with the German NSU Motorcycle Company. He was designing a small car. He built three prototypes. These cars were the original models of the Beetle. They were called Type 32s.

Adolf Hitler wanted a car for the average German citizen. Hitler wanted this car to be able to carry two adults and three children.

Adolf Hitler wanted to mass-produce a vehicle for the German people.

He wanted this car to have a top speed of 62 miles (100 kilometers) per hour. He also wanted this car to be able to drive 33 miles per gallon (13 kilometers per liter) of gas. Above all, Hitler wanted a car the average worker could afford. He wanted this car to cost less than $400 (1,000 German marks).

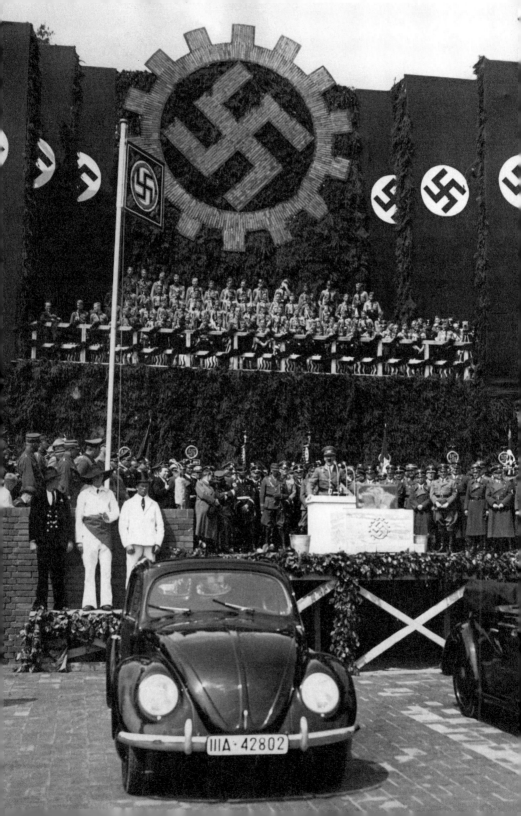

At the time, only one out of every 48 Germans could afford to own a car. In the United States, one in every five people owned a car.

Hitler liked the design of the Type 32. In 1934, he hired Porsche to build the "people's car."

In 1937, Porsche built the VW38 model of the Beetle. Hitler test-drove this car and approved its design. In 1938, he ordered a factory to be built in Wolfsburg, Germany, to produce the VW38.

The VW38 had a four-cylinder engine. Cylinders are the hollow metal tubes in an engine where gas is burned. This engine produced 30 horsepower and gave the VW38 a top speed of 65 miles (105 kilometers) per hour. Horsepower is a measure of an engine's power.

Effects of World War II

The German government ordered Porsche to build military vehicles at the Wolfsburg factory. He designed tanks, airplane engines, and transport vehicles to carry soldiers. Porsche used designs of the Beetle to build many of these

---

Adolf Hitler ordered a factory to be built in Wolfsburg, Germany, that would produce the Beetle.

military vehicles. One such vehicle was the Type 166. This vehicle was an amphibious jeep. The Type 166 could travel on land and in water. It floated and had a small propeller on the back. This spinning metal blade helped the Type 166 move through water.

Early in 1945, Germany surrendered to the allied forces. The Wolfsburg factory had been bombed by British and U.S. airplanes. Much of the machinery in the factory was damaged. Production at the factory stopped.

The Beetle

In June 1945, production at the Wolfsburg factory began again. Between 1945 and 1946, the Wolfsburg factory produced more than 10,000 Beetles. In 1947, it produced nearly 9,000 Beetles.

After World War II, the United States gave money to Germany to help rebuild its factories. This program was called the Marshall Plan. In 1948, Heinz Nordhoff was hired as general director of the Wolfsburg factory. He improved

Ferdinand Porsche used the Beetle's design to build many military vehicles during World War II.

the factory with money from the Marshall Plan. Production at the Wolfsburg factory increased to more than 19,000 vehicles in 1948.

Nordhoff began to sell Beetles in other countries. In 1948, Beetles were sold in Belgium, Luxembourg, and Switzerland. In 1949, the first Beetle was shipped to the United States. By 1952, Beetles were sold in Canada.

Chapter 3

The Beetle Years

In 1955, Volkswagen produced its 1 millionth Beetle. To celebrate, the company held a party at the Wolfsburg factory in Germany. The party was for factory workers and the car dealers who sold Beetles. About 140,000 people attended this celebration.

Many people bought Beetles in the 1950s and 1960s. Volkswagen built more factories to keep up with the demand. In 1960, it opened a factory in France. In 1965, it opened a factory in Mexico.

Volkswagen sold a record number of Beetles. Between 1908 and 1927, the Ford Motor Company built more than 15 million Model Ts. No car company had ever made

The Beetle is the world's best-selling car model ever.

Volkswagen increased the Beetle's engine size and improved its suspension system.

more cars of one model. In 1972, the Beetle broke this record. Volkswagen eventually produced more than 21 million Beetles.

Some Changes to the Beetle

In 1954, Volkswagen increased the size of the Beetle's engine. Older models had an engine that was nearly 69 cubic inches (1,131 cubic centimeters). This measurement is the space inside the engine's cylinders where gas is burned. The old Beetle engine produced 30 horsepower. Volkswagen increased the engine size to nearly 73 cubic inches (1,192 cubic centimeters). The larger engine produced 36 horsepower.

In 1958, Volkswagen added larger front and rear windows to the Beetle. This gave drivers a better view of traffic. In 1961, Volkswagen increased the trunk size in all Beetle models. The trunk then had more room to carry luggage. In 1964, Volkswagen added seats with vinyl coverings to the Beetle. This waterproof material is easier to clean than fabric.

The 1971 Super Beetle was a much improved model of the Beetle. It had a larger engine. The Super Beetle's engine was nearly 97 cubic inches (1,584 cubic centimeters) and produced 60 horsepower. This model also had an improved suspension system. The suspension system includes the springs and shock absorbers that support vehicles on their wheels. Vehicles with a good suspension system ride more smoothly. It also is easier for drivers to steer a vehicle with a good suspension system.

Restoring the Beetle

Car collectors restore old cars. They find parts for these cars and fix them. Collectors search for engine parts. They look for fabric for the insides of cars. They even look for radio knobs.

Parts for old cars can be difficult to find. Many older models are no longer produced. Many old cars have been destroyed by rust. Old cars also may have parts that no longer work. Beetles are easier to restore than most cars because many Beetles were made. This makes parts easier to find.

Fun with the Beetle

Some people do more than just restore their Beetles. They customize their cars. They paint their cars in unusual ways and decorate them. People who customize their Beetles often join clubs. Club members show each other how they have restored and customized their Beetles.

Some Beetle owners convert their Beetles into race cars. These owners put bigger engines in their cars. For example, Jim Kelso drag races his Beetle. A drag race is a short race driven on

Many owners of old Beetles like to display their vehicles at old car shows.

a straight stretch of road. Kelso's car *Shutterbug* has a 461-cubic-inch (7,554-cubic-centimeter) engine that produces 500 horsepower. Other owners race their Beetles off road. These cars are called baja beetles.

During the 1960s, many college students owned Beetles. Some students made up a game called Volkestote. Teams of students would carry Beetles 100 yards (91 meters) from a starting line. Then everyone on a team would get inside their Beetle and drive it back to the starting line.

Chapter 4

The New Beetle

During the 1970s, countries around the world passed stronger air pollution laws. Some of these laws controlled how much pollution cars could produce. The Beetle did not pass U.S. pollution standards. After 1981, new models of the Beetle could not be sold in the United States. Some European governments also did not allow Beetles to be sold in their countries. Only the Volkswagen factory in Mexico still produced Beetles. Beetles were still sold in Mexico. Mexico's pollution laws were not as strict as the laws in the United States and many European countries.

In 1994, Volkswagen displayed Concept 1 at the North American International Auto

The new Beetle was designed for today's auto market.

/20688

Concept 1 was built to look like the original Beetle designed by Ferdinand Porsche.

Show in Detroit, Michigan. This new model of the Beetle passed modern pollution and safety laws.

The Beetle Engine

The new Beetle is different from the old Beetle in several ways. The old Beetle had an air-cooled engine. Air from outside the engine flows through the engine to keep it cool. The modern Beetle's engine is water cooled. Water flows through rubber tubes to keep the engine cool. A water-cooled engine produces less pollution than an air-cooled engine.

The new Beetle's engine also is more powerful. Its engine produces 115 horsepower. Its top speed is 113 miles (182 kilometers) per hour.

Safety Features

The new Beetle has an anti-lock braking system (ABS). A computer controls this braking system and keeps the brakes from locking. This gives drivers better control of their cars when braking. Brakes on cars without ABS can lock when drivers brake quickly. This stops vehicles' wheels from spinning. Drivers cannot control or steer their vehicles easily if the wheels are not spinning.

New Beetles have air bags. Air bags inflate when a vehicle crashes. They help protect the driver and front-seat passenger. One air bag is located in the steering wheel. Another is located in the vehicle's dashboard in front of the front-seat passenger.

New Beetles also have side-impact air bags. These air bags protect drivers and passengers when cars are hit from the side.

All cars are tested for safety. This insures that they pass modern safety laws. The Institute for Insurance & Highway Safety (IIHS) is one company that tests the safety of cars. In 1998, IIHS ranked the new Beetle as the safest small car in the United States.

Other Changes to the Beetle

The new Beetle has options that were not included in the old Beetle. Some of these options are leather seats, air conditioning, and beverage holders.

The new Beetle is sold as a "2 plus 2" automobile. It has two small seats in back. But these seats are only big enough for children or to store luggage.

Air bags inflate like balloons to protect the driver and front-seat passenger.

The new Beetle also has an improved suspension system. It steers more easily and has a smoother ride than the old Beetle.

Nostalgic Appeal

The design of the Beetle is not completely new. Today's Beetle is built to look like the old Beetle. Both are small cars with curved front ends and roofs. Their dashboards also look similar. Both cars have one round speedometer in front of the driver.

Many older models of the Beetle are still being driven today.

Volkswagen hopes the modern Beetle will appeal to people who owned an old Beetle.

Volkswagen hopes to use nostalgic appeal to sell the new Beetle. The old Beetle was a very popular car. Volkswagen designed the new Beetle to look like the old Beetle. Volkswagen hopes some of the people who liked the old Beetle will buy the new Beetle.

The New Volkswagen Beetle

Parts of an Engine

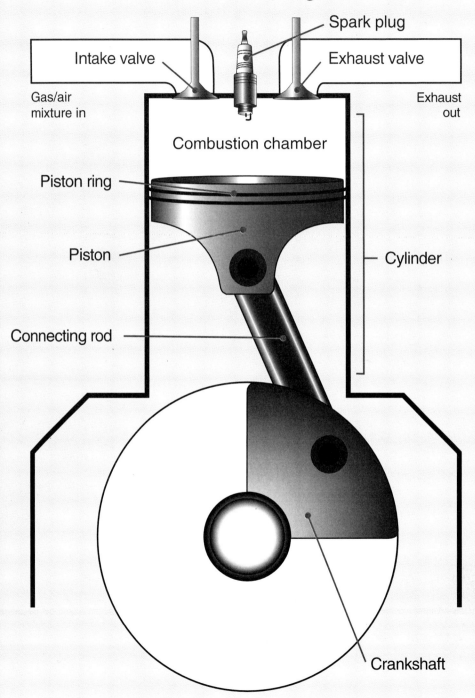

Spark plug

Intake valve

Exhaust valve

Gas/air mixture in

Exhaust out

Combustion chamber

Piston ring

Piston

Cylinder

Connecting rod

Crankshaft

Quick Facts about Engines

Most cars and trucks have internal combustion engines. Internal combustion engines create power by burning gasoline inside the engines. This power turns the wheels of vehicles. Internal combustion engines also are used in motorcycles and lawn mowers.

Parts of an Internal Combustion Engine

Cylinder: The cylinder is a hollow metal tube in the engine. A lawn mower has one cylinder. Most cars and trucks have four, six, or eight cylinders.

Internal combustion engines are used in cars, trucks, motorcycles, and lawn mowers.

Combustion chamber: The combustion chamber is the space inside the cylinder. A gas and air mixture is burned in the combustion chamber.

Intake valve: Gas and air enter the combustion chamber through a hole in the top of the cylinder. The intake valve opens and closes this hole. A cylinder usually has one intake valve.

Exhaust valve: Exhaust leaves the combustion chamber through a hole in the top of the cylinder. The exhaust valve opens and closes this hole. A cylinder usually has one exhaust valve.

Spark plugs: Spark plugs light the gas and air mixture in the combustion chamber. This makes the mixture burn.

Piston: The piston is a round piece of metal that moves up and down in the cylinder.

Piston rings: Piston rings stop air, gas, and smoke from leaking out of the combustion chamber.

The original model of the Beetle had its engine in the rear of the car.

Crankshaft: The up-and-down motion of the piston spins the crankshaft. This spinning motion applies power to the wheels of a vehicle.

Connecting rod: The connecting rod connects the piston to the crankshaft.

The Engine Cycle

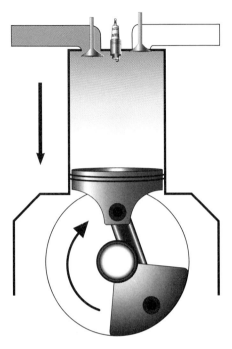

1. Intake
The piston moves down and the intake valve opens. Air and gas enter the combustion chamber.

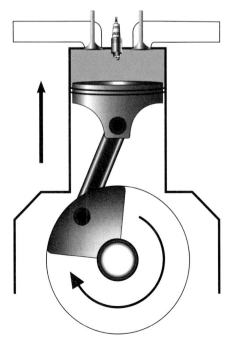

2. Compression
The intake valve closes. The piston then moves up. This upward movement forces the air and gas into a smaller space. This action is called compression. Compression also pushes the mixture of air and gas into contact with the spark plug.

3. Combustion

The spark plug lights the air and gas mixture. The burning gas and air pushes the piston down.

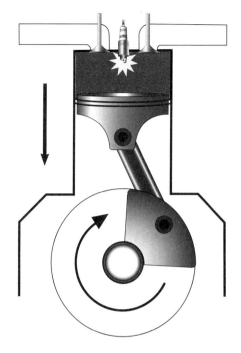

4. Exhaust

The exhaust valve opens. The piston moves up. This pushes burned gas out of the combustion chamber.

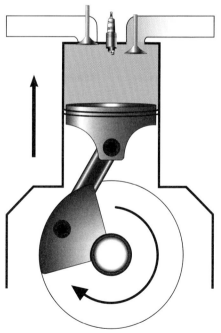

The four stages in the engine cycle are intake, compression, combustion, and exhaust.

The Power of an Engine

Engines create power by burning gas. Engines that burn more gas in each cycle create more power. People can do two things to make engines burn more gas. They can add more cylinders to engines. They also can make the cylinders bigger.

Horsepower is a measurement of an engine's power. One horsepower is the force needed to move 33,000 pounds (14,969 kilograms) a distance of 12 inches (30 centimeters) in one minute.

Cars with more powerful engines can often reach faster speeds. The original Beetle's engine could produce only 30 horsepower. This car had a top speed of 65 miles (105 kilometers) per hour. The new Beetle has an engine that produces 115 horsepower. Its top speed is 113 miles (182 kilometers) per hour.

A larger engine gives the new Beetle more horsepower and a faster top speed.

Words to Know

air bags (AIR BAGSS)—a safety feature that inflates like a balloon; air bags protect the driver and front-seat passenger in a crash.

amphibious jeep (am-FIB-ee-uss JEEP)—a vehicle that can travel both on land and in water

anti-lock brake system (AN-tee-LOK BRAYK SISS-tuhm)—a braking system controlled by a computer; an anti-lock brake system prevents brakes from locking.

baja beetle (BAH-hah BEE-tuhl)—a beetle customized to race off road

concept car (KON-sept KAR)—a car that displays an automaker's new ideas for a car model

drag race (DRAG RAYSS)—a race on a short, straight road

horsepower (HORSS-pou-ur)—the measure of an engine's power

internal combustion engine (in-TUR-nuhl kuhm-BUSS-chuhn EN-juhn)—an engine that creates power by burning gasoline inside

nostalgic (noss-TAL-jik)—to like what is old; people like the new Beetle because it has similarities to the old Beetle.

options (OP-shuhnss)—extra features on a car

prototype (PROH-tuh-tipe)—the test car of a new car model

suspension system (suh-SPEN-shuhn SISS-tuhm)—the system of springs and shock absorbers that supports a vehicle

vinyl (VYE-nuhl)—easy-to-clean, waterproof material often used for seat covers

Volkswagen (VOHLKSS-wag-uhn)—German automaker; Volkswagen means "people's car" in German.

To Learn More

Baaske, Edwin. *Volkswagen Beetle: Portrait of a Legend.* Cambridge, Mass.: Robert Bentley Publishers, 1997.

Burgan, Michael. *The Porsche 911.* On the Road. Mankato, Minn.: Capstone Press, 1999.

Nelson, Walter Henry. *Small Wonder: The Amazing Story of the Volkswagen Beetle.* Cambridge, Mass.: Robert Bentley Publishers, 1998.

Seume, Keith. *VW Beetle: A Comprehensive Illustrated History of the World's Most Popular Car.* Osceola, Wis.: Motorbooks International Publishers & Wholesalers, 1997.

Useful Addresses

Maritime Volkswagen Owners Club
2279 Amirault Street
Dieppe, NB E1A 7K6
Canada

Vintage Parts Inc.
317 North Victory Boulevard
Burbank, CA 91502

VW Club
VW Club Headquarters
P.O. Box 2012
Bloomfield Hills, MI 48303-2012

Internet Sites

The Beetle Farm
http://www.thebeetlefarm.com/index2.htm

Concept 1 - The New Beetle
http://www.beetle.de

The New Beetle
http://www3.vw.com/cars/newbeetle

VW Club
http://www3.vw.com/owners/club.htm

Index